Antichrist, Armageddon, and the Mark of the Beast
Antichrist's Identity Revealed

Henry Bechthold

When citing scripture in this book I have quoted from the New King James Version of the Bible.

Contents

Chapter One

Antichrist and the "Unholy Trinity" Revealed

The Antichrist, Armageddon and the mark of the beast are probably the three most researched topics in the book of Revelation. This book will do a detailed scriptural examination of each of these subjects. From the biblical evidence revealed, you will discover that there is a lot of "misinformation" being promulgated by many so-called prophecy experts, especially regarding the Antichrist and Armageddon. I will be presenting numerous scriptures that are being ignored by these prophecy teachers. We will begin our study with the Antichrist.

All Bible students know that the Antichrist will be an evil being who will be under the control of Satan.

However, beyond that, there are various ideas about exactly who he will be, where he will come from, and about how and when he will arrive. Fortunately, the Bible specifically answers the questions of who the Antichrist will be, and of where he will come from. As to how and when he will arrive, this is not quite as clear in Scripture. But, a thorough study of the book of Revelation, combined with an awareness of the deceptions of Satan that are gaining in popularity in our culture, can enable us to make a reasonable, biblical, educated guess as to how and when the Antichrist will arrive.

You cannot do a biblical examination of the Antichrist without also including Satan as part of that study, because they are directly related. And, as you will discover from the scriptures presented in this chapter, a "third" *evil being* also needs to be included in our study of the Antichrist. This *evil being* is referred to as "another beast" in Revelation 13:11, and as the "false prophet" in Revelation 16:13. We will begin our study with the following scripture from the book of Isaiah.

In Isaiah 14:12-14, the Bible states, "(12) How you are fallen from heaven, O Lucifer, son of the morning! How you are cut down to the ground, you who weakened the nations! (13) For you have said in your heart: "I will ascend into heaven, *I will exalt my throne above the stars of God*; I will also sit in the mount of the congregation on the farthest sides of the north; (14) I will ascend above the heights of the clouds, *I will be like the Most High*."

Of course, all who have studied the Bible know that "Lucifer" was Satan's name before he rebelled in heaven and was cast down to the earth. Why have I listed this scripture about Lucifer to begin our biblical examination of the Antichrist? Because this text gives us insight into how this whole "sin and evil" mess began, and it also gives us insight as to what was the "core issue" at the heart of Lucifer's (Satan's) rebellion. In this passage, Lucifer (Satan) stated that he wanted to exalt his throne above the stars of God; he said, "I will be like the Most High". In other words, Satan wanted to be God. And, as you will see, Satan tries to "pull it off" in the final days of Earth's history.

As stated in the previous paragraph, Satan wants to be God. In Isaiah 14:14, he said that he wanted to become "like" the Most High. And, Satan knows that God is a "trinity". Therefore, in the culmination of events on planet Earth, Satan will establish his own "false trinity", an **unholy** *trinity*.

We know that the "true trinity", the "holy trinity", consists of God the Father, God the Son (Jesus Christ) and the Holy Spirit. Thus, Satan attempts to establish a precise counterfeit of Almighty God's trinity here on earth, where Satan himself stands at the head of this **unholy trinity** as the "**unholy** god the father". Satan is referred to as the "dragon" in the book of Revelation. And, Revelation reveals that this dragon, Satan, is the one in charge of this unholy trinity; it states that he is the one who gives the beast or Antichrist his power, throne and authority. Note the following two scripture passages.

In Revelation 12:3-9, the Apostle John stated, "(3) And another sign appeared in heaven: behold, a great, *fiery red dragon* having seven heads and ten horns, and seven diadems on his heads. (4) *His tail drew a third of the stars of heaven and threw them to the earth. And the dragon stood before the woman who was ready to give birth, to devour her Child as soon as it was born.* (5) She bore a male Child who was to rule all nations with a rod of iron. And her Child was caught up to God and His throne. (6) Then the woman fled into the wilderness, where she has a place prepared by God, that they should feed her there one thousand two hundred and sixty days. (7) ***And war broke out in heaven***: Michael and his angels fought with the dragon; and the dragon and his angels fought, (8) but they did not prevail, nor was a place found for them in heaven any longer. (9) ***So the great dragon was cast out, that serpent of old, called the Devil and Satan, who deceives the whole world; he was cast to the earth, and his angels were cast out with him***."

In Revelation 13:1-4, John declared, "(1) Then I stood on the sand of the sea. And I saw a beast rising up out of the sea, having seven heads and ten horns, and on his horns ten crowns, and on his heads a blasphemous name. (2) Now the beast which I saw was like a leopard, his feet were like *the feet of* a bear, and his mouth like the mouth of a lion. ***The "dragon" gave him his power, his throne, and great authority***. (3) And I saw one of his heads as if it had been mortally wounded, and his deadly wound was healed. And all the world marveled and followed the beast. (4) ***So they worshiped the "dragon" who gave authority to the beast***; and they worshiped the beast, saying, "Who *is* like the beast? Who is able to make war with him?"

We have already learned that Satan's rebellion began in heaven while he was still named Lucifer, when he decided that he wanted to be God. The passage in Revelation chapter twelve revealed that Satan's prideful rebellion resulted in the fall of one-third of the "stars" or "*angels*" in heaven who apparently chose to follow Satan; note that Jesus used the term "stars" to represent angels in Revelation 1:20. Per Revelation 12:7-9, Satan's prideful rebellion also led to "war in heaven" where Satan and his evil angels fought against God's mighty angel Michael and God's holy angels, and Satan and his evil angels were defeated and thrown out of heaven, being cast down to the Earth. Revelation 12:9 not only identified the dragon as being the Devil or Satan, but also called him "that *serpent of old*". Why? Because it was Satan who spoke through a serpent in the Garden of Eden when he tempted Eve, and caused the "fall of mankind".

You see, Satan has always been the one heading the rebellion against God, and leading both angels and men into sin and evil. He started his *evil crusade* in heaven, and has continued it here on earth. He has always been the "one in charge" when it comes to evil and rebellion against God. And, in Earth's final days,

Satan is again at the head of the final rebellion. The Revelation 13:1-4 passage stated that it is the dragon Satan who will give the Antichrist Beast his power, throne and authority. So, in the midst of Earth's final rebellion in the days of Antichrist, Satan is still in control, serving as the "*unholy* god the father" of his *unholy trinity*. Note the following two scriptures.

In 2nd Corinthians 4:3-4, the Apostle Paul proclaimed, "(3) But even if our gospel is veiled, it is veiled to those who are perishing, (4) whose minds the *"god" of this age* has blinded, who do not believe, lest the light of the gospel of the glory of Christ, who is the image of God, should shine on them."

In John 8:44, Jesus said to the Jewish leaders, "You are of *your "father" the devil*, and the desires of *your "father"* you want to do. He was a murderer from the beginning, and does not stand in the truth, because there is no truth in him. When he speaks a lie, he speaks from his own *resources,* for *he is a liar and the "father" of it*."

In the passage in 2nd Corinthians, we see the Apostle Paul mentioning the "*god* of this *age* or *world*", depending on your Bible translation, as having blinded people's minds to the gospel of Christ. Who is the one who is working to blind people to the gospel? Of course, that is Satan. Therefore, in this text, Paul refers to Satan as the "***god***" of this age or world. And, in the John 8:44 passage, Jesus calls Satan the "***father*** of lies" and also the "***father***" of the wicked Jewish leaders who rejected Jesus. So, in the Scriptures, Satan is referred to as both a "***god***" and a "***father***", with both of these references being used in an evil and "unholy" context. Thus, I am biblically correct in referring to Satan as the ***unholy god the father*** in Satan's unholy trinity.

We will now discuss the second member in Satan's trinity, the Antichrist. Whereas Satan is the "unholy god the father" in his evil trinity, the Antichrist is the ***unholy christ*** or "unholy god manifest in the flesh". This will be biblically proven through the examination of numerous scriptures. We will now begin an in depth Bible study about the Antichrist.

It should be noted that the Antichrist is referred to as the "beast" throughout the book of Revelation. We know that this "beast" represents the Antichrist because, in Revelation chapter 13, this beast is worshipped and followed by the whole world; he blasphemes God and makes war against God's saints; he is mortally wounded, but his deadly wound is healed; he has an image built to him, which all people are commanded to worship, and those who don't are killed; all people are forced to receive a "mark" in their right hand or forehead that contains the beast's name or number, 666, or they will not be able to buy or sell. This "beast" in the book of Revelation clearly is the Antichrist.

But, what type of *being* is this Antichrist? Is he a man? Is he a demon? And, where will the Antichrist come from? Will he come from a particular nation or continent? Note the following scriptures.

Revelation 17:8 states, "The ***beast (Antichrist)*** that you saw was, and is not, and ***will ascend out of the "bottomless pit"*** and go to perdition. And those who dwell on the earth will marvel, whose names are not written in the Book of Life from the foundation of the world, when they see the beast that was, and is not, and yet is."

Revelation 11:7 says, "When they finish their testimony, the ***"beast" (Antichrist) that ascends out of the "bottomless pit"*** will make war against them, overcome them, and kill them."

Both of these scriptures state that the "beast" or "Antichrist", from henceforth I will often just say Antichrist, will ascend out of the ***bottomless pit*** or "abyss", depending on your Bible translation. The original Greek word used by the Apostle John is the word "abussos". The literal meaning of this Greek word is "a deep or bottomless pit or abyss". This word is very significant, because it will help answer the questions of who the Antichrist is, and where he is from. Please note the following scriptures which also use this Greek word, "abussos".

In Revelation 20:1-3, the Apostle John declared, "(1) Then I saw an angel coming down from heaven, having the key to the *"bottomless pit"* and a great chain in his hand. (2) *He laid hold of the dragon, that serpent of old, who is the Devil and Satan*, and bound him for a thousand years; (3) and *he cast him into the "bottomless pit"*, and shut him up, and set a seal on him, so that he should deceive the nations no more till the thousand years were finished. But after these things he must be released for a little while."

In Luke 8:30-31, the Bible states, "(30) Jesus asked him, saying, "What is your name?" And he said, "Legion", because many demons had entered him. (31) And they begged Him that He would not command them to go out into the *abyss*."

In the first passage, Revelation 20:1-3, the *bottomless pit* or "abyss" mentioned in this text is translated from the Greek word "abussos". And, this scripture states that it is the place where Satan will be chained for 1000 years.

In the second passage, Luke 8:30-31, the **bottomless pit** or "abyss" or "deep", depending on your Bible translation, which is referred to in this scripture, is again translated from the Greek word "abussos". And, this text reveals that it is a place that the demons named "legion" **begged Jesus** not to cast them into. Therefore, these demons were obviously familiar with this place, and they also obviously must have known that it was a place of torment. And, the only way that they could have known that, is if other demons (fallen angels) had previously been cast into the **abussos**.

There is another significant scripture which also uses this word, "abussos", in Revelation chapter nine. I ask you to read Revelation 9:1-11.

In this passage, Revelation 9:1-11, as stated in the previous paragraph, once again it is the Greek word "abussos" that is translated as **bottomless pit** or **abyss**. And, this text states that it is the place that will be unlocked during the fifth trumpet, from which hordes of "demon locusts" will be released, with a fallen angel named Abaddon or Apollyon as king of these *demon locusts*. In chapter three I will discuss these locusts in greater detail, proving that they are indeed demons.

So, per these last three scripture passages, what type of beings dwell in, or are cast into, the ***abussos***? Per these texts, the answer is, Satan, demonic locusts, and demons or fallen angels in general. It is highly significant that human beings are **never** said to dwell in, or be cast into, the ***abussos*** in the entire Bible. Therefore, we can conclusively state that the "abussos" is a place occupied solely by Satan and his demons or fallen angels.

Now that we know that the ***abussos*** is a place occupied solely by the demonic realm, what does this tell us about the Antichrist? Remember that Revelation 11:7 and Revelation 17:8 stated that the Antichrist Beast will *ascend* out of the "abussos", the bottomless pit or abyss. If the *abussos* is only filled with demonic beings, and Antichrist comes from the *abussos*, then we know that Antichrist is a "demon" or "fallen angel".

We have answered the question of where the Antichrist comes from. He comes from the ***abussos***. And, knowing that, we also know that the Antichrist is a ***demon***. So, have we therefore also answered the question of who the Antichrist is, a "demon"? Actually, we have only "half" answered that question. Note the following scripture regarding the Antichrist Beast.

In Revelation 13:18, the Apostle John declared, "Here is wisdom. Let him who has understanding calculate the number of the *beast*, for *it is the number of a "man"*: His number is 666."

This passage states that the Antichrist Beast has a number, 666. And, it says that it is the "number of a *man*". Thus, per this scripture, the Antichrist is a "man". However, the other texts we just examined revealed the Antichrist to be a "demon".

How can the Antichrist be both a demon and a man? This brings us back to my earlier statement that the Antichrist is the second member of Satan's "Unholy Trinity". He is the "False Christ", the "*Unholy Christ*", the unholy god manifest in the flesh. Jesus Christ is the *God Man*, and the antichrist is the *demon man*. Is this possible? From the following scriptures, you will see that it is very possible, in fact *probable*. Note the following scripture from the book of Genesis.

Genesis 6:1-5 states, "(1) Now it came to pass, when men began to multiply on the face of the earth, and daughters were born to them, (2) that the **sons of God** saw the **daughters of men**, that they *were* beautiful; and they took wives for themselves of all whom they chose. (3) And the Lord said, "My Spirit shall not strive with man forever, for he *is* indeed flesh; yet his days shall be one hundred and twenty years." (4) There were **giants** on the earth in those days, and also afterward, ***when the sons of God came in to the daughters of men and they bore children to them***. Those *were* the mighty men who *were* of old, men of renown. (5) Then the Lord saw that the wickedness of man *was* great in the earth, and *that* every intent of the thoughts of his heart *was* only evil continually."

This passage stated that the "sons of God" went into the "daughters of men", and that **giants** were born of them, followed by such an immediate and drastic increase of wickedness that ***every intent and thought*** of the people was "wicked continually", except for Noah and his family. This incredible *spike* in wickedness happened within just 1500 years of a "perfect creation" *starting point*. We have not replicated that level of evil in the 4500 years since then, and our *starting point* was from an "imperfect Noah", not a *perfect* Adam and Eve in the Garden of

Eden. So, something out of the ordinary must have happened to radically increase the level of evil so quickly and dramatically.

The reference to the "sons of God" *going into* the "daughters of men" in this passage is very significant. The traditional explanation given by many preachers has been that these *sons of God* represent righteous men, and that the *daughters of men* represent unrighteous women; thus, they say that this scripture is just saying that righteous men had sexual relations with unrighteous women. There are, however, three problems with this explanation. Would truly *righteous men* be having sexual relations with unrighteous women? And, why would "righteous men" having sexual relations with unrighteous women cause **giants** to be born, and cause such a great and immediate increase of evil, the likes of which we have never seen since then? Moreover, I cannot think of any other reference in Scripture when a righteous man married or had sexual relations with an unrighteous woman, where it is referred to as a "son of God" having *gone into* a "daughter of men". This is, in fact, a very unique passage, and I believe it has a very unique answer, which is a biblical answer. Note the following four scriptures which also use this expression, "sons of God".

In Job 1:6, the Bible states, "Now there was a day when the *sons of God* came to present themselves before the Lord, and Satan also came among them."

In Job 2:1, the Bible says, "Again there was a day when the *sons of God* came to present themselves before the Lord, and Satan came also among them to present himself before the Lord."

In Job 38:4-7, God declared to Job, "(4) Where were you when I laid the foundations of the earth? Tell Me, if you have understanding. (5) Who determined its measurements? Surely You know! Or who stretched the line upon it? (6) To what were its foundations fastened? Or who laid its cornerstone, (7) when the morning stars sang together, and all the *sons of God* shouted for joy?"

In Luke 20:34-36, the Bible states, "(34) Jesus answered and said to them, "The sons of this age marry and are given in marriage. (35) But those who are counted worthy to attain that age, and the resurrection from the dead, neither marry nor are given in marriage; (36) nor can they die anymore, for they are *equal to the angels* and *are "sons of God"*, being sons of the resurrection."

In the first two passages, Job 1:6 and Job 2:1, there were some type of *meetings* or *assemblies* being held someplace in God's vast created universe, other than Earth. I say, "other than Earth", because, in Job 1:7 and Job 2:2, God asked Satan where he had come from, and in both instances Satan said that he had come ***from Earth*** to attend these meetings or assemblies. However, for our purposes, we are focused on the statement in both of these verses that the "sons of God" had come to present themselves before the Lord on both of these occasions. Who would these "sons of God" be? We know that it is not human beings from Earth, because the fallen angel Satan is representing Earth. These are obviously some type of "heavenly" or ***angelic beings***. And, being that Satan, a fallen ***angel***, is described as being ***among them***, it would not be unreasonable to assume that the "sons of God" were all ***angelic beings***. In fact, the NIV translation actually refers to these *beings* as "angels", rather than as "sons of God".

In the Job 38:4-7 passage, God asked Job where he was when God was creating the Earth, fastening its foundations and determining its measurements. And, God mentions in verse seven, that the ***sons of God*** were shouting for joy while He was creating the

Earth. Once again, these "sons of God" cannot be referring to human beings, because human beings had not been created yet. Therefore, this must again be referring to some type of *angelic beings*. And, as with the other two scriptures in Job, the NIV translation again refers to these *beings* as "angels", rather than as "sons of God".

In the passage in Luke, Jesus stated that the resurrected saints who enter heaven, will have become "equal to the angels", being ***sons of God***. So, per Jesus' statement, being ***equal to the angels***, equals being "sons of God". I do need to mention that the original King James and NIV translations render Luke 20:36 as "children" of God, rather than "sons" of God. However, the New King James, New American Standard and Amplified Bible translations render this verse as "sons" of God. The original Greek word used in this verse is "huios", which is used 382 times in the New Testament. Out of those 382 times, it is translated as "son" 329 times, which is 86% of the time. So, there is an 86% chance that the correct translation is "sons" of God, and only a 14% chance that it should *children* of God.

In all of these scripture passages, the expression, "sons of God", appears to equate to ***angels***.

Therefore, at the very least, it is certainly a plausible biblical option for us to consider the possibility of the reference to **sons of God** going into the **daughters of men**, as referring to angels *mingling* with women. And, because the fallen angel Satan was considered to be one of those "*sons of God*", we know that this term also includes "fallen angels". So, it is possible, if not probable, that Genesis 6:1-5 is referring to fallen angels or demons having sexual relations with women, which certainly would explain why the level of evil had such a great and immediate increase. And, there are also other indications in Scripture that this indeed could be the case. Note the two following scriptures.

In Jude verses 6-7, the Apostle Jude said, "(6) And the angels **who did not keep their proper domain**, **but left their own abode**, He has reserved in everlasting chains under darkness for the judgment of the great day; (7) as Sodom and Gomorrah, and the cities around them in a similar manner to these, having given themselves over to "sexual immorality" and gone after "strange flesh", are set forth as an example, suffering the vengeance of eternal fire."

In 2nd Peter 2:4, Peter stated, "For if God did not spare **the angels who sinned**, **but cast them down to** *"hell"* and delivered them into chains of darkness, to be reserved for judgment;….."

The passage in Jude mentioned ***angels*** who did not keep their ***proper domain***, and who "left their abode". And, because these angels did this, God put them in everlasting chains under darkness until the judgment. The passage in 2nd Peter basically adds to Jude's description, saying that God cast the angels who "sinned" down to "hell". The Greek word translated as hell in this text is "tartaros". This is the only time that this Greek word, "tartaros", is used in the entire Bible. It literally means "***deepest abyss***". Also, people are **never** referred to as being in, or going to, "tartaros". Therefore, when combining the message of these two scriptures in Jude and 2nd Peter, this ***deepest abyss*** was only for a group of fallen angels who ***sinned*** by leaving their "proper domain". Could this be referring to the "sons of God" or ***fallen angels*** in Genesis chapter six, who disobeyed God by having sexual relations with women, trying to totally pollute and destroy the human race, in an effort to quickly and drastically increase sin to such an extent that human minds would be totally taken over by sin, which then resulted in God casting these fallen angels into this "deepest abyss"? At this point, we need to take another look at Jude verses 6-7, but this time we will be primarily focusing on verse seven. For your convenience, I have listed this scripture again below.

Jude 6-7 states, "(6) And the angels *who did not keep their proper domain*, *but left their own abode*, He has reserved in everlasting chains under darkness for the judgment of the great day; (7) *as Sodom and Gomorrah*, and the cities around them *in a "similar manner" to these*, *having given themselves over to "sexual immorality" and gone after "strange flesh"*, are set forth as an example, suffering the vengeance of eternal fire."

Jude verse seven adds more biblical support for this theory regarding fallen angels sexually mingling with women. Why? Because right after mentioning the angels who did not keep their "proper domain" and who "left their abode" in verse six; verse seven immediately follows with the statement that Sodom and Gomorrah, in a "similar manner", gave themselves over to *sexual immorality* and going after *strange flesh*. Jude verse seven, clearly states that Sodom and Gomorrah's sins of "sexual immorality" and going after "strange flesh", were *similar* to the sins of the fallen angels in verse six. Therefore, we know that these angels' sins were of a "sexual nature" with "strange flesh". This reference makes it highly probable that a number of fallen angels did indeed engage in sexual relations with women, which would have been ***strange flesh*** to angels. Note the following scripture, which we briefly discussed before, but now need to reexamine.

Luke 8:30-31 says, "(30) Jesus asked him, saying, "What is your name?" And he said, "Legion", because many demons had entered him. (31) And they begged Him that He would not command them to go out into the ***abyss***."

This passage makes this theory even more likely. As previously stated, when Jesus was casting out the demons named "Legion", they begged Him not to cast them into the "abussos", the *abyss* or *bottomless pit*. So, these demons were obviously aware of a very "unpleasant" place where fallen angels or demons could be cast into. How did they know this unless some of their fellow "fallen angels" had already been sent there, such as the ones who sinned by not keeping their proper domain when they, the *sons of God* in Genesis 6:1-5, had sexual relations with women?

It is noteworthy that the ***abussos***, abyss or bottomless pit, is never mentioned as a place where people enter, just as ***tartaros***, deepest abyss, is also never referred to as a place where people enter. It seems likely that these two words are referring to the same place, because, as previously mentioned, you can't get any deeper of an abyss than a bottomless one; furthermore, because both words refer to the location where disobedient fallen angels are punished.

As you can see, there is a strong biblical case that can be made that fallen angels had sexual relations with women, creating a combination "demon man" offspring, which *only had evil thoughts continually*, as stated in Genesis 6:5; furthermore, resulting in these fallen angels being cast into a place of torment referred to as the "abussos" and "tartaros", a *deepest abyss* or *bottomless pit*.

At this time we need to do a quick review of a few significant things we've learned, before moving on. In Revelation 20:1-3, we found that the *abussos* is the place where Satan will be cast into for a thousand years. In Revelation 9:1-11, we discovered that the *abussos* is the place that will be unlocked during the fifth trumpet, and from which hordes of "demon locusts" will be released. And, in Luke 8:30-31, we learned that the *abussos* is also the place that demons begged Jesus not to cast them into, probably based on their knowledge of this place of torment due to many of their *fallen angel friends* having been cast into it after having had sexual relations with women (Genesis 6:1-5; Jude 6-7; 2nd Peter 2:4). In these passages, Scripture makes it clear that the *abussos* is a place occupied only by the "***demonic realm***"; moreover, there are no scriptures in the entire Bible which state that human beings are ever put into the *abussos*.

In Revelation 11:7 and Revelation 17:8 we discovered that the *abussos* is also the place where the Antichrist will ascend from. And, knowing that the *abussos* is occupied solely by the ***demonic realm***, we therefore learned that the Antichrist is a "demon". In the process of learning these things, we also discovered when the Antichrist will arrive on Earth, which will be during the sounding of the fifth trumpet, because the *abussos* is not unlocked until the fifth trumpet, and the Antichrist comes forth from the *abussos*.

So, the Antichrist is a ***demon*** who will not appear until the sounding of the fifth trumpet, which means that the Antichrist will not be present on Earth during the first four trumpets, which we will examine in chapter three. However, we also found, in Revelation

13:18, that the Antichrist is also a "man". This passage stated that the Antichrist Beast has a number, 666. And, it said that it is the "number of a *man*"; thus meaning that the Antichrist is a "man".

Therefore, the Scriptures indicate that the Antichrist is both a "demon" and a "man". How can he be both demon and man? Could he be one of the wicked "demon men" offspring from Genesis chapter six, thus making him the perfect *wicked counterfeit* for Jesus Christ in Satan's unholy trinity; Jesus being the holy "God Man" offspring, and the Antichrist being the unholy "demon man" offspring? It is interesting and significant that the Greek word, "abussos", is only used one other time in the Bible, and that is in the following scripture.

In Romans 10:6-7, the Apostle Paul declared, "(6) But the righteousness of faith speaks in this way, "Do not say in your heart, who will ascend into heaven?" (that is, to bring Christ down from above) (7) or, "Who will descend into the *abyss*?" (that is, to bring Christ up from the dead).

This passage states that Jesus went into the *abyss*, Greek word "abussos", while He was dead. I need to note that the original King James and NIV translations render the word *abussos* as the "deep", instead of **abyss**, in this scripture. However, the New King James, New American Standard and Amplified Bible translations all render "abussos" as **abyss** in this text. But, regardless of how various translations choose to translate this Greek word in this verse, the only thing that matters is that the original Greek word chosen by the Holy Spirit is "abussos". Per this scripture, Jesus went into the *abussos* while He was dead.

Why would Jesus have gone into the **abussos**, where only fallen angels or demons, and apparently also their "demon men" offspring are located? Why would Jesus have gone there, and what did He do there? Note that, I included the "demon men" offspring as being in the *abussos*, because we know that the Antichrist was also there, who is called a man while still having been one of the demons in the *abussos*. Furthermore, because this evil **tainted offspring** would have been "half" demon, they would not simply die and lie in the grave, because demons or fallen angels **do not die**, so it is probable that these "half demons" would have been kept in the same place as the "full demons" or fallen angels who *fathered* them, that being the **abussos**. My statement that angels do not die is scripturally documented in my book, "Sadistic Teachings In The Church; The Scriptural Evidence Refuting The Doctrines Of Eternal Punishment and Calvinism". You can purchase the e-book for only 99 cents at Amazon.

This statement in Romans 10:7, that Jesus went into the *abussos* while He was dead, will lead us down a scriptural trail that is both interesting and very significant. Note the two following scriptures.

In 1st Peter 3:18-20, the Apostle Peter said, "(18) For Christ also suffered once for sins, the just for the unjust, that He might bring us to God, being put to death in the flesh but made alive *by the Spirit*, (19) *by whom also He (Christ) went and "preached" to the "spirits in prison"*, (20) *who formerly were disobedient*, when once the Divine longsuffering waited *in the days of Noah*, while *the* ark was being prepared, in which a few, that is, eight souls, were saved through water."

In Ephesians 4:8-10, Paul states, "(8) Therefore He says: "When He ascended on high, *He led "captivity captive"*, and gave gifts to men." (9) (Now this, "He ascended"—what does it mean but that *He also first "descended" into the "lower parts" of the Earth*? He who descended is also the One who ascended far above all the heavens, that He might fill all things.)"

The first passage, 1st Peter 3:18-20, stated that Christ, through the Spirit, went and **preached** to some "spirits in prison", who had been disobedient ***during the days of Noah***. Who could these "spirits in prison" that had been disobedient in the days of Noah be?

The second passage, Ephesians 4:8-10, referred to Christ having "descended" into the ***lower parts*** of the earth, before ascending on high while *leading* "captivity captive", as stated in the original King James and New King James translations. The NIV and New English Bible translations say, "He led captives in His train". And, the Revised Standard and New American Standard Bible translations state, "He led a host of captives". The obvious consensus of these various translations is that this Ephesians text is clearly stating that Jesus returned from His visit to the "lower parts" of the earth with a group that had apparently been held captive there, whom Jesus took with Him when He "ascended on high". Who could these "captives" that had been held in the ***lower parts*** of the Earth be?

Could it be that Christ's infinite love, grace, mercy and equitable justice caused Him to give an opportunity for salvation to those who had no opportunity before, because they had "demonic genes" mingled with human genes resulting from the intercourse of fallen angels with the daughters of men, which had caused their thoughts to be evil continually, as stated in Genesis 6:1-5? And, were these "demon men" offspring in Genesis, the "spirits in prison" from the days of Noah that the Bible says Christ preached to in 1st Peter 3:18-20?

At His death, did Christ's spirit descend into the "lower parts" of the earth mentioned in Ephesians 4:8-10, into the *"abussos"* referred to in Romans 10:7, where He *preached*, as stated in 1st Peter 3:19, the gospel to this "tainted offspring" in such a manner that they would also have an opportunity for salvation? And, did many or perhaps most of them accept the gospel; thus constituting the "host of captives" that Christ victoriously took captive to Himself when He ascended back to heaven, as stated in Ephesians 4:8? It all certainly seems to add up scripturally.

Then, could it be possible that Satan will choose to exalt one of the remaining "demon men" offspring to the position of being the second person in his "***unholy trinity godhead***", because this "demon man" had maintained his fidelity to Satan, by refusing the gospel message preached by Christ, and also because his combined *"demon man"* status makes him the perfect **unholy counterfeit** of Jesus' combined *"God Man"* status? And now, after having been locked away in the dreaded *"abussos"* for more than 4000 years, he is among those who are released when the *abussos* is unlocked during the fifth trumpet, per Revelation 9:1-11. Therefore, he comes out with such a ferocious vengeance, hatred and malevolence against Jesus, that he relishes the idea of stealing Christ's glory by impersonating Him; moreover, that causes him to want to exterminate all those who call on the name of Jesus Christ.

This scenario, with the Antichrist imitating Christ's supernatural "God Man" status, by being an evil, supernatural *"demon man"*, accords with Scripture. And, there is a passage in the Book of 2nd Thessalonians that gives additional evidence of Antichrist's attempt to duplicate the role of Jesus Christ. I encourage you to read 2nd Thessalonians 2:1-10.

If you read this text, you saw that it mentioned a *person* or *being* referred to as the "man of sin" or "man of lawlessness", the "son of perdition" or "man doomed to destruction", depending on your Bible translation, and also referred to as the "lawless one".

This **being** is universally understood to be the Antichrist. And, this text states that the Antichrist will claim to be God, even as Jesus claimed to be equal with God in John 5:18, and claimed to be the "I AM" (God) in John 8:58, which gives evidence of the Antichrist's "imitation" of Jesus Christ. Also note the following scripture in the Book of Revelation, which gives additional evidence of the Antichrist's attempt to duplicate the role of Jesus Christ.

In Revelation 13:2-4, John stated, "(2) Now the **beast** (**Antichrist**) which I saw was like a leopard, his feet were like *the feet of* a bear, and his mouth like the mouth of a lion. ***The "dragon" gave him his power, his throne, and great authority***. (3) And ***I saw one of his heads as if it had been "mortally wounded", and his "deadly wound" was healed. And all the world marveled and followed the beast*** (**Antichrist**). (4) ***So they worshiped the dragon who gave authority to the beast***; and they worshiped the beast, saying, "Who *is* like the beast? Who is able to make war with him?"

This passage states that the ***dragon*** (Satan), who is the "unholy god the father" of his *unholy trinity*, will give Antichrist his power and authority, even as Jesus said that His Father gave Him His authority and power to do the works that He did, in John 14:10-11.

This text also said that the Antichrist Beast will receive a "mortal" or "deadly" wound, but he will revive, even as Jesus died on the cross and was resurrected.

It is indeed obvious from Scripture, that the Antichrist is an attempted *evil duplicate* of Jesus Christ; Jesus Christ being the holy "God Man" in the sacred *biblical trinity*, and the Antichrist being the unholy "demon man" in Satan's *unholy trinity*. So, if the dragon or Satan is the *"unholy god the father"* in Satan's false and *unholy* trinity; and if the Antichrist is the second person in this *unholy trinity*, the "demon man" or *unholy god manifest in the flesh*; then, who is the third person of Satan's evil trinity? Who is his replacement for the Holy Spirit? It is the *second beast* that appears in Revelation chapter 13, referred to as "another beast" in Revelation 13:11, and also referred to as the "false prophet" in Revelation 16:13. Note the two following passages.

In Revelation 13:11-17, John declared, "(11) Then I saw *another beast* coming up out of the earth, and he had two horns like a *lamb* and *spoke like a "dragon"*. (12) And he exercises all the authority of the first beast in his presence, and causes the earth and those who dwell in it to worship the first beast, whose deadly wound was healed. (13) *He performs great signs*, so that he even makes fire come down from heaven on the earth in the sight of men. (14) And he deceives those who dwell on the earth by those signs which he was granted to do in the sight of the beast, telling those who dwell on the earth to *"make an image" to the beast (Antichrist)* who was wounded by the sword and lived. (15) He was granted *power* to *give "breath" to the image of the beast, that the image of the beast should both "speak"* and cause as many as would not worship the image of the beast to be killed. (16) He causes all, both small and great, rich and poor, free and slave, to receive a mark on their right hand or on their foreheads, (17) and that no one may buy or sell except one who has the mark or the name of the beast, or the number of his name."

In Revelation 16:13-14, John stated, "(13) And I saw *three unclean spirits* like frogs coming out of the mouth of the dragon, out the mouth of the beast (Antichrist), and out of the mouth of the *"false prophet"*. (14) For they are *spirits of demons*, performing signs, which go out to the kings of the earth and of the whole world, to gather them to the battle of that great day of God Almighty."

The passage in Revelation 13:11-17 reveals that this second beast, referred to as "another beast" in verse eleven, will look like a *lamb*, but he will speak like a *dragon*. We know that Jesus Christ is the "*Lamb* of God" in Scripture, and we know that the dragon represents Satan. Therefore, this second beast entity must pretend to be "lamb like" or *Christ like*, but his words and his commands come straight from Satan. This text states that he has the same authority as the "first beast", Antichrist, in his presence, and he does miracles to deceive the world in order to cause people to worship the Antichrist. He has an "image", apparently a *statue* or *idol*, made to the Antichrist, and he miraculously causes this "icon" to *breathe* and *speak*. Then, everyone is commanded to worship this idol, and if they don't, they will be killed.

We are talking about full blown idolatry here. How could this happen in our 21st century world? I believe that we live in a world that is prepared to believe in and worship such a "talking image" as the one presented in Revelation chapter 13. More than three billion Muslims, Hindus and Buddhists are already accustomed to worshipping and bowing to supposedly "sacred places" and/or *religious statues*. And, more than one billion Roman Catholics throughout the world have been bowing to and revering religious statues for many centuries. And, in recent times, some Catholic *icons* have been mysteriously and miraculously weeping tears or oozing oil or blood, resulting in their veneration and worship; these things are preparing Roman Catholics throughout the world to also accept and worship such a t*alking image.*

Why do I say that this *second beast* of Revelation chapter 13 is Satan's replacement for the Holy Spirit in Satan's "unholy trinity"? There are several reasons. This *second beast* is also called the "false prophet", in the second passage I listed, Revelation 16:13-14. And, of course, prophecy is one of the gifts of the **Holy Spirit**. Also, whereas the Antichrist Beast is referred to as a "man" in Revelation 13:18, the second beast of Revelation chapter 13, the "false prophet" of Revelation 16:13-14, is never referred to as a *man*, just as the Holy Spirit is not a man. Could this "false prophet" be the *exact opposite*, the **complete counterfeit** of the Holy Spirit; nothing more than one of Satan's demons, the *"unholy spirit"*, impersonating a human prophet? And, could it be possible that his impersonation will take on the form of the prophet Mohammed having returned to earth, so as to secure the support of earth's nearly two billion Muslims? Also consider the following scriptures.

In John 15:26, John said, "But when the Helper comes, whom I shall send to you from the Father, *the Spirit of Truth* which proceeds from the Father, *He will testify of Me*."

In John 16:13-14, John stated, "(13) However, when He, *the Spirit of Truth*, has come, He will guide you into all truth; for He will not speak on His own authority, but whatever He hears He will speak; and He will tell you things to come. (14) *He will glorify Me*, for He will take of what is Mine and declare it to you."

These two scriptures from the Gospel of John state that the Holy Spirit testifies of Jesus and glorifies Him. And, Revelation chapter 13 stated that the second beast, the "false prophet" of Revelation chapter 16, also testifies of the Antichrist Beast and glorifies and exalts him to the extent of causing the world to worship him. So, we see again that the second beast, the "false prophet", attempts to do the same thing for the Antichrist, as the Holy Spirit does for Jesus Christ.

In Acts 1:8, Jesus proclaimed, "But *you shall receive "power" when the "Holy Spirit" has come*

upon you; and you shall be witnesses to Me in Jerusalem, and in all Judea and Samaria, and to the end of the earth."

In 1st Corinthians 12:10-11, regarding the gifts of the Holy Spirit, Paul declared, "(10) to another ***the working of miracles***, to another prophecy, to another discerning of spirits, to another different kinds of tongues, to another the interpretation of tongues. (11) But one and ***the same "Spirit" works all these things***, distributing to each one individually as He wills."

In these two texts from the books of Acts and 1st Corinthians, we see that the Holy Spirit provides ***power*** and ***powerful gifts***, like the "working of miracles". And, likewise, Revelation 13:13-14 states that the second beast, the *false prophet* of Revelation chapter 16, also works miracles, performing "great signs" and making fire come down from heaven. Once again, the second beast of Revelation chapter 13, the *false prophet*, mimics the Holy Spirit by also working miracles.

This "second beast" of Revelation chapter 13, also known as the "false prophet", is indeed an apparent counterfeit for the Holy Spirit; Satan's "unholy spirit". Thus, Satan's ***unholy trinity*** is complete. However, as always, Satan comes up short in his effort to copy God's "holy trinity". We're told in Revelation 13:18 that Satan's number is "666". However, God's special number in the Bible is the number "seven", also commonly referred to as God's "perfect number". And, because God is a trinity, it would not be incorrect to say that God's *trinity number* is "777". Satan comes up short again.

Chapter Two

A Seven Year Reign of Antichrist?

Most of the so-called prophecy experts today teach that the Antichrist will reign over the world for seven years. However, there are not any scriptures in the entire Bible which specifically say that this is the case; not a single text in all of Scripture states that the Antichrist reigns for seven years. In fact, the book of Revelation specifically states that the Antichrist reigns for forty two months, which would be three and one-half years. And yet, this seven year reign of the Antichrist is a widely accepted doctrine in the contemporary Christian Church. But do not be surprised by this. There is also no true scriptural support for several other doctrines commonly taught in today's Church, such as the popular "secret" or "pre-tribulation" rapture, and yet this doctrine is also widely accepted in the contemporary Christian Church. I have written another book titled, "Seeker Sensitive Doctrines That Can Take You To Hell", in which I discuss this "secret" or "pretribulation" rapture doctrine. In this book I list dozens of scriptures which clearly and totally refute this false teaching. This book is available at Amazon for only 99 cents in e-book format; a paperback version is also available. Also, a little later in this book, in chapter four, you will discover that the widely taught "Battle of Armageddon" doctrine, with all the nations of Earth gathering together to fight one another, with some fighting against the nation of Israel, and with some fighting against Antichrist himself, is also clearly and completely contradicted and refuted by the book of Revelation. And these are not the only doctrines commonly taught in today's Church which clearly contradict Scripture. In my book, "Babylon Is Fallen, Come Out Of Her My People", which is also available at Amazon, several other false doctrines are exposed. As I said before, do not be surprised by the promulgation of all of these false and unscriptural doctrines in the contemporary Church, because the Apostle Paul warned that the time would come when this would happen. Note what Paul said in the following scripture.

In 2nd Timothy 4:1-4, Paul declared, "(1) I charge *you* therefore before God and the Lord Jesus Christ, who will judge the living and the dead at His appearing and His kingdom: (2) *Preach the "word"*! Be ready in season *and* out of season. Convince, rebuke, exhort, with all longsuffering and teaching. (3) *For the time will come when they will NOT endure "sound doctrine"*, but according to their own desires, *because* they have itching ears, they will heap up for themselves teachers; (4) *and they will turn their ears away from the "truth", and be turned aside to "fables".*"

In this passage, Paul told Timothy to keep preaching only "the Word", the Scriptures. Paul instructed Timothy to do this "in season", *when convenient*, and "out of season", *when not convenient*. In some settings with some groups of people it is easy or convenient to preach the truth in God's Word; there is no danger of rejection or persecution. However, there are also settings with other groups of people where the truth in God's Word is not welcome; settings where it is hard and inconvenient to preach the Word; settings where the messenger will be rejected, persecuted, and hated for proclaiming the straight truth from the Bible.

Paul stated that the time will come when they "will not endure *sound doctrine*". Remembering the context in this passage in 2nd Timothy, that this statement immediately follows Paul's commission to "preach the Word", even when *not convenient*; it is apparent that the "sound doctrine" being referred to in verse three of this passage, would be doctrines grounded in and based on "the Word", Scripture, mentioned in verse two. In other words, Paul was warning us that the day would come when doctrines in the Church would no longer be built solely upon the Scriptures; that time is here.

Paul went on to say that there will be teachers who turn people away from the "truth", and who will turn them to "fables" instead. Jesus said in John 17:17, "Thy Word is truth". Therefore, Paul was stating that the day will come when teachers will arise who will abandon the Word, the Bible, as the one and only source of doctrine, and who will rather teach "fables" instead; that day is here.

The Greek word that is translated as fables in this passage is the word "muthos", meaning a "*tale, fiction, myth* or *fable*". The Strong's Expanded

Exhaustive Concordance gives the following expanded definition of this Greek word: "*Muthos* is that which is a simple account, which attempts to explain reality; yet is unreal and *fabricated*, having only the appearance of truth, no truth actually contained therein."

So, per this Greek definition, this passage in 2nd Timothy is stating that teachers will arise who will teach mere "fabrications of men", which they claim to be explaining reality, and which they try to make appear as being true; however, there is no truth in these fabrications or fables. Fabrications are things that are "made up". So, per this Strong's Concordance definition, these teachers will be teaching "made up doctrines" and presenting them as truth, but there is no truth in them. Wow! This Scripture in 2nd Timothy 4:1-4 is being fulfilled before our eyes today with the assortment of false doctrines being taught in the contemporary Church.

Now, back to the focus of this chapter, the *supposed* seven year reign of Antichrist. Note the two following passages in the book of Revelation.

In Revelation 11:1-7, the Bible states, "(1) Then I was given a reed like a measuring rod. And the angel stood, saying, "Rise and measure the temple of God, the altar, and those who worship there. (2) But leave out the court which is outside the temple, and do not measure it, for it has been *given to the Gentiles*. And *they will tread the holy city underfoot for "forty two months"*. (3) And *I will give power to my two witnesses, and they will prophesy "one thousand two hundred and sixty days {1260 days or 42 months}", clothed in sackcloth*." (4) These are the two olive trees and the two lampstands standing before the God of the earth. (5) And if anyone wants to harm them, fire proceeds from their mouth and devours their enemies. And if anyone wants to harm them, he must be killed in this manner. (6) These have power to shut heaven, so that no rain falls in the days of their prophecy; and they have power over waters to turn them to blood, and to strike the earth with all plagues, as often as they desire. (7) When they finish their testimony, *the beast {Antichrist} that ascends out of the bottomless pit will make war against them, overcome them, and kill them*."

In Revelation 13:4-7, the Bible declares, "(4) So they worshiped the dragon who gave authority to the beast; and they worshiped the *beast {Antichrist}*, saying, "Who *is* like the beast? Who is able to make war with him?" (5) And he was given a mouth speaking great things and blasphemies, and *he was given authority to continue for "forty two months"*. (6) Then he opened his mouth in blasphemy against God, to blaspheme His name, His tabernacle, and those who dwell in heaven. (7) *It was granted to him to make war with the saints and to overcome them.* And authority was given him over every tribe, tongue, and nation."

The second scripture, Revelation 13:4-7, specifically states that the Antichrist beast is in authority for "forty two months", which equals *three and one-half years*, NOT "seven" years. You can't make it any clearer than that. And, it says that, during this time period, he makes war with the "saints", God's people, and overcomes them.

The first scripture, Revelation 11:1-7, mentioned this same time period of "forty two months", as a time when the *holy city* will be tread underfoot by the "Gentiles", which can also be translated as "nations", "ethnic groups", or "races". Because of this, per Revelation 11:3, God's "two witnesses", which I scripturally prove to be converted Jewish and Gentile Christians in my book titled, "The Book Of Revelation, False Prophetic Teachings Exposed", which is also available at Amazon; these two witnesses will be conducting their prophetic ministry clothed in sackcloth, and the time period for their ministry is said to be 1260 days, which again equals forty two months. Of course, God's witnesses being clothed in "sackcloth" during this time period, depicts hard and sorrowful times. And, this would certainly be the case, as Antichrist is persecuting them, making war with them, and overcoming them, as stated in Revelation 11:2, Revelation 11:7, and Revelation 13:7. But, for our purposes in this chapter, we once again see that Antichrist's reign is "forty two months", "1260 days", equaling *three and one-half years*, NOT "seven" years. As clearly stated in Revelation 13:5, "he (the Antichrist beast) was given authority to continue for "forty two months"."

With such clear statements in the book of Revelation, that the Antichrist is only in authority for forty two months, three and one-half years, how do these prophesy teachers try to support their "seven year reign" doctrine? They do so by *manipulating* Daniel's seventy week prophecy regarding Israel and the Messiah, in Daniel 9:24-27. This scripture follows.

Daniel 9:24-27 states, "(24) Seventy weeks are determined for your people and for your holy city, to finish the transgression, to make an end of sins, to make reconciliation for iniquity, to bring in everlasting righteousness, to seal up vision and prophecy, and to anoint the Most Holy. (25) Know therefore and understand, that from the going forth of the command to restore and build Jerusalem until Messiah the Prince, there shall be seven weeks and sixty two weeks; the street shall be built again, and the wall, even in troublesome times. (26) And after the sixty two weeks Messiah shall be cut off, but not for Himself; and the people of the prince who is to come shall destroy the city and the sanctuary. The end of it shall be with a flood, and till the end of war desolations are determined. (27) Then He shall confirm a covenant with many for one week; but in the middle of the week He shall bring an end to sacrifice and offering. And on the wing of abominations shall be one who makes desolate, even until the consummation, which is determined, is poured out on the desolate."

As previously stated, the idea of a seven year reign of Antichrist was arrived at by "manipulating" Daniel's seventy week prophecy concerning Israel and the Messiah, in the passage you just read, Daniel 9:24-27. Daniel's prophecy states that "seventy weeks" were determined for his people, the Jews, and for Jerusalem, to make an end of their sins, to bring in everlasting righteousness, and to anoint the "Most Holy", the Messiah. The "start date" of the prophecy is declared to be when the command was given to restore and build Jerusalem; this command was given by the Persian King Artaxerxes in 458 BC. We know that it was in the year 458 BC, because Ezra 7:7-9 states that these things happened in the seventh year of the Persian King Artaxerxes' reign, which would be 458 BC. Why? Because history reveals that Artaxerxes' reign began during the year of 465 BC, which means that the first full year of his reign began in 465 BC and ended during 464 BC. Thus, the seventh year of his reign included 458 BC. Most theologians and Bible commentaries agree that the 70 weeks, equaling 490 days, in Daniel's prophecy, represent 490 years. However, far more important than the consensus of theologians, we do also have a biblical example of God using a day for a year in prophecy. Note the following scripture.

In Numbers 14:34, God said, "According to the number of the days in which you spied out the land, forty days, for each day you shall bear your guilt one year, namely forty years, and you shall know My rejection."

In this passage, God prophesied to Israel that they would spend 40 years wandering in the wilderness, which He said was *a year for each day* that they had spent spying the land of Canaan. And indeed, as God had said, Israel did spend forty years in the wilderness, thus fulfilling what God had prophetically stated. Therefore, it is scriptural to equate the 490 days in Daniel's prophecy to 490 years.

Now remember, Daniel 9:24-27 said that these 490 years were given to the Jews to make an end of their sins, to establish righteousness, and to *"anoint" the "Most Holy"*, the Messiah. Daniel's prophecy states that there would be *7 weeks plus 62 weeks* until the coming of "Messiah the Prince"; in other words, *69 weeks* equaling 483 days or "years". Adding 483 years onto the start date of Artaxerxes' decree brings us to 26 AD. What happened in 26 AD? Jesus was baptized by John the Baptist and anointed with the Holy Spirit in the form of a dove descending upon Him from Heaven, as recorded in Luke 3:21-22. Luke 3:1 states that this happened in the *fifteenth year* of Tiberius Caesar, which was 26 AD. How do we arrive at this date? Because historical records reveal that he began his co-reign in 11 AD. However, per Roman law, the first year was considered to be a "year of succession", and was not counted as the first year of a new emperor's reign. Thus the first year of his actual reign would have been 12 AD. And, if 12 AD is year one of Tiberius' reign, then 26 AD would be year fifteen of his reign. History and prophetic timing matched perfectly! The conclusion of the 69th week of Daniel's prophecy brings us exactly to that 26 AD date when Jesus was anointed with the Holy Spirit and began His public ministry. However, Daniel said that a total of 70 weeks were determined for Israel to stop their sinning and to establish righteousness. And Daniel 9:27 states that, following the first 69 weeks, "He", which in proper context is the Messiah (Jesus Christ), would still confirm His covenant for one more week, which would have to be the 70th week. And it states that, in the middle of that 70th week, "He" (the Messiah) would bring an end to sacrifice and offering.

This is where most of today's prophecy teachers "manipulate" Scripture, by taking this 70th week and arbitrarily separating it from the previous 69 weeks, and placing it 2,000 years in the future, into the 21st century. Furthermore, they change the context, which

Daniel had clearly stated applied to the Messiah, Jesus Christ, but they now apply this 70th week *to* "Antichrist", in order to fit into their prophetic paradigm. If we are allowed to split prophetic time prophecies at our own choosing, breaking certain portions of the prophecy off, and inserting them hundreds or thousands of years later at our own discretion; then, we can pretty much concoct any fulfillment of Scripture that pleases us. Likewise, if we are allowed to arbitrarily switch the "subject" of texts from the Messiah, Jesus Christ, to Antichrist, once again, it allows mere men to manufacture their own personal favorite fulfillment of prophecy. If Daniel had wanted the 70th week of his seventy week prophecy separated by 2,000 years, he would have said so. Furthermore, this prophecy finds a remarkably precise fulfillment when leaving the seventy weeks "intact" as Daniel wrote it.

Remember that Daniel 9:24 stated that 70 weeks, which equals 490 days, "490 years" in prophecy, were determined for Daniel's people, the Jews, to "finish their transgression", to make an "end of their sins", and to bring in righteousness. When adding the 70th week, which would equal 7 days, "7 years" *prophetically*, onto 26 AD, it brings us to 33 AD.

What happened in 33 AD? The first recorded Christian martyr in the New Testament was a man named Stephen, who was stoned for his witness and testimony for Christ, as recorded in Acts 7:58-60. Acts chapter six describes Stephen as being full of faith, power, and the Holy Spirit, and who did signs and wonders among the people. While the exact year of his stoning cannot be proven with 100% certainty, most church theologians and historians estimate his martyrdom to have occurred somewhere from 33 AD to 36 AD. However, it is interesting, and perhaps significant, that "St. Stephen's Day" is celebrated on December 26 every year in Ireland, and they teach that Stephen was stoned in 33 AD, which would be exactly at the end of Daniel's seventy week prophecy. And this celebration and recognition of Stephen's martyrdom for Christ goes back many hundreds of years in Ireland. I believe it is a "safe bet" that Stephen was indeed martyred in 33 AD, because that is the exact year when Daniel's 490 year time prophecy ends, and all of the other dates of this prophecy have been biblically and historically proven. Thus it is reasonable to assume that the final date associated with this prophecy would be accurate as well. It is certainly significant that immediately following Stephen's martyrdom, Acts 8:1-5 records that the Jews, through Saul of Tarsus, greatly persecuted the Christian Church and made havoc of it, which resulted in the Church scattering "everywhere" preaching the word, as stated in Acts 8:4. Philip even went to the *hated* Samaritans preaching the gospel. And, from then on, throughout the book of Acts, the gospel message is taken primarily to the Gentiles. The Jews' 70 week "probationary period" thus ended in 33 AD. The fact that the gospel was primarily taken to the Gentiles, and primarily believed and received by the Gentiles, is evidenced by the fact that, out of the 2.3 billion Christians in the world today, only about 400,000 of them are Messianic Jews. This means that for each and every Christian Jew in the world today, there are 5,750 Christian Gentiles.

There is another astounding prophetic fulfillment of Daniel 9:27. Daniel states that, in the "middle" of that 70th week, "He", which in proper context is the Messiah, would bring an end to sacrifice and offering. The middle of the 70th week would be about half way between 26 AD and 33 AD. That would have to be either 29 AD or 30 AD.

What happened at that time? Most early church historians date Jesus' death anywhere from 30 AD to

33 AD. We know from Scripture that Jesus was crucified on a Friday, and that He was crucified on the Passover, which means that there was a "full moon". It certainly seems to be more than a coincidence that in the year 30 AD, which is in the middle of the 70th week of Daniel's prophecy, astronomical data reveals that there was indeed a full moon on Passover Friday. This must be when Jesus, the true Lamb of God, was offered on the "altar" of the "cross", which made any future offerings of lambs and other animal sacrifices meaningless. These sacrifices had been mere *types* and *symbols* of the true reality, the true fulfillment, the *antitype* that was to come, Jesus Christ. Therefore, Jesus' death on the cross, as the true Lamb of God, ended the sacrificial system from God's standpoint. Jesus had truly *brought an end to sacrifice and offering*, as Daniel's prophecy stated. This was graphically demonstrated by God when the veil of the temple separating the "Holy Place" from the "Most Holy Place" was supernaturally torn in two as Jesus died on the cross, as stated in Matthew 27:50-51. God's presence was no longer abiding in the Jewish temple, so the "Most Holy Place" no longer needed to be separated by a veil. This clearly indicated that the Jewish temple, its

services and sacrifices, were now empty and meaningless, for Christ had fulfilled everything represented by them. And, in remarkable fulfillment of Daniel's prophecy, it happened in 30 AD, *in the middle of the 70th week*.

With such extraordinary fulfillments of Daniel's prophecy when the 70 weeks are left "intact", how did theologians come up with the idea of removing the 70th week and placing it 2,000 years in the future, and also switching the "subject" of the prophecy from the Messiah, Jesus Christ, to the Antichrist? Who originally did this? It was done in the sixteenth century by a Roman Catholic, Jesuit priest named Francisco Ribera in his 500 page commentary on the book of Revelation titled, "In Sacrum Beati Ioannis Apostoli & Evangelistiae Apocalypsin Commentarij". Ribera was the first one to separate the 70th week of Daniel's prophecy and to place it in the distant future, which planted the foundation for the *secret rapture* or *pretribulation* doctrine, as well as the seven year reign of Antichrist, instead of the three and one-half years clearly taught in Scripture, in Revelation 13:5 and Revelation 11:1-7.

How or why did this Roman Catholic, Jesuit priest come up with this "futuristic" 70th week doctrine?

Quite simply, it was to protect the papacy from the charges of Protestant reformers that the Pope himself was the Antichrist. In the Council of Trent in the mid sixteenth century, the papacy decided to search for ways to prove that the Pope could not be the Antichrist. Francisco Ribera put forth his doctrine of placing Daniel's 70th week in the distant future, with the Antichrist's reign occurring in that time frame, thus also attempting to prove that the Pope could not be the Antichrist. Thus, the foundations of today's popular, but unbiblical, secret rapture or pretribulation doctrine, and the seven year reign of Antichrist teaching, were laid by a Roman Catholic Jesuit priest who was trying to protect the papacy.

We have completed our examination of the doctrine of the seven year reign of Antichrist, and we have found this teaching to be totally, 100% unbiblical. We have seen that scriptures have been manipulated in an effort to support this false teaching. The Bible is clear that the reign of Antichrist is three and one-half years, "not" seven years.

At the end of this chapter, I need to note that, while it is true that there was also a full moon on Passover Friday in 33 AD, and this date has been made popular as the crucifixion date through "The

Star of Bethlehem" DVD, and the bethlehemstar.net website; there are, however, serious biblical, historical, and chronological errors made by the author of this DVD regarding the 33 AD date. These errors are documented in my e-book titled, "The Star of Bethlehem DVD Refuted: And the False Doctrine of the 7-Year Reign of Antichrist Exposed". This e-book is available at Amazon for just 99 cents. My book titled, "Four More False Doctrines And Practices", available in paperback and e-book, also exposes these errors in "The Star Of Bethlehem" DVD.

Chapter Three

How Will Antichrist Arrive?

One of the undeniable quandaries regarding the Antichrist is, how will he arrive in such a way and at such a time that will make Jews, Christians, Hindus, Buddhists, and Muslims all be willing to accept this same man as their mutual leader? If he arrives as a Jew or a Christian, the other major world religions will reject him. Likewise, if he arrives as a Hindu or a Buddhist, he will be rejected by the Muslims, Christians and Jews. And, if he arrives as a Muslim, he will receive the same rejection from the other religions. How can he arrive in a manner that will make 500 million Buddhists, more than two billion Christians, one billion Hindus, nearly two billion Muslims, and millions of Jews all welcome him as their mutual leader? His appearance will obviously have to involve some apparently supernatural or miraculous signs in order to attain this worldwide acceptance throughout all of Earth's major world religions.

Also, what world conditions will need to be present for all of Earth's nations to accept him as the leader of one worldwide global government? There will need to be some critical and common "global problems" that require common *"global solutions"*. Four of these worldwide "global problems" already exist. Even now, we have a common, global, pandemic medical problem, and it will not be the last; we have a common, global economic crisis caused by the pandemic, which also will not be the last; we have a perceived common, global warming climate problem; and, although things have been calmer recently, for the past few decades we have had a common, global terrorism problem, which is likely to resurface at some point in the future. Furthermore, we have been, and already are, working toward common, global solutions to these four problems, including a global shift toward governments taking great oversight, control and/or ownership of banks throughout the world, which will lay the foundation for a global monetary system and, eventually, a worldwide *cashless society*.

However, it will take more than just these four causes to bring about worldwide acceptance of a one world government under Antichrist. It will require far more urgent and desperate circumstances throughout the world, as well as the humbling of three *superpowers*: the United States, China and Russia. I believe that this will be accomplished by the "fifth global cause", which is the catastrophic, supernatural calamities accompanying the angelic blowing of the first five trumpets recorded in chapters eight and nine in the book of Revelation. These are divine judgments poured out on a wicked world in the final days of earth's history. I ask you to read Revelation 8:2-13 and Revelation 9:1-11

Revelation 8:7 stated that the *first trumpet* will bring hail and fire mingled with blood upon the Earth to the extent that one-third of Earth's trees will be burned up, as well as the grass. This judgment is similar to the seventh plague poured out on Egypt in the days of Moses, which also had hail and fire mingled. The reference to fire accompanying the hail probably indicates severe and widespread lightning that ignites the fires that burn Earth's trees and grass.

These must be ferocious storms that encompass most of the world, because one-third of Earth's foliage is destroyed. The description of blood mingled with the hail and fire probably depicts the great loss of life caused by the hail, lightning, and winds from this incredible global storm.

Per Revelation 8:8-9, the *second trumpet* will cause a "great mountain" that is *on fire* to be cast down to the Earth, which will destroy one-third of the ships in the sea (ocean) and will kill one-third of the sea creatures, while causing one-third of the sea (ocean) to become like blood. This is an obvious depiction of a large asteroid, perhaps miles in diameter, which would indeed have the appearance of being a mountain on fire falling from the sky. The bloodlike appearance of the ocean could be from discoloration caused by the asteroid or, more likely, is a graphic illustration of the blood that will be shed by the millions of people who will be killed when one-third of Earth's ships are destroyed, combined with one-third of Earth's sea life also perishing. It is apparent that this asteroid will land in one of Earth's great oceans, probably the Atlantic or Pacific, in order to cause this degree of loss.

Revelation 8:10-11 stated that the *third trumpet* will cause a "great star" burning like a torch to fall from heaven, which will result in one-third of Earth's rivers and springs of water becoming *wormwood*, probably meaning that they will become exceedingly bitter, undrinkable and poisoned. It states that this tainted water will result in the death of many men. This certainly cannot be referring to a literal, physical star that falls to Earth, because one star falling upon the Earth could only affect the rivers and springs where it actually fell. To poison one-third of Earth's rivers and springs would require thousands of stars falling throughout the world. Therefore, this "great star" is obviously symbolic. And, we know that the term *star* is used elsewhere in the book of Revelation to represent angels, as in Revelation 1:20 and Revelation 12:4-9. So, this third trumpet probably depicts a great angel coming down from heaven to turn one-third of Earth's rivers and springs into "wormwood" as another judgment upon our rebellious world. Now, at this point, the Earth will have been pummeled by a global hailstorm, set on fire by the lightning from this storm, devastated from the impact of a huge asteroid, and had one-third of its fresh water sources poisoned and undrinkable.

Millions of dead bodies will be everywhere, and disease will be widespread throughout the world. Furthermore, multitudes will be dying from thirst and starvation. It is fair to say that chaos and panic will be rampant.

Per Revelation 8:12, the *fourth trumpet* will bring darkness to one-third of the sun, moon and stars. This could either be a supernatural miracle of God, or the natural result of the previous trumpets. Scientists tell us that one of the aftereffects of a major asteroid colliding with Earth would be numerous earthquakes followed by massive volcanic eruptions sending incredible volumes of volcanic ash into our atmosphere, which, when combined with the smoke from fires already covering one-third of Earth's surface, would certainly result in darkness covering much of our planet, probably the equivalent of one-third, as stated in Revelation 8:12. Whatever the cause, one-third of the world will now be covered in darkness.

In the *fifth trumpet*, described in Revelation 9:1-11, the key to the *bottomless pit* will be given to a "star" *fallen from heaven*. Since literal, physical stars do not have hands to receive or use keys, it is reasonable to assume that this *star* is also symbolic of an angel; in this case, a "fallen" angel named Abaddon or Apollyon, as stated in Revelation 9:11. This angel will use this *key* to open the "bottomless pit". The Greek word used here is "abussos", which literally means an abyss or *bottomless pit*, as stated earlier in this book. As you will see, this is quite significant.

When the ***abussos*** is opened a dark smoke arises, from which comes "demonic locusts". Why do I call them *demonic locusts*? There are several reasons. As previously mentioned in this book, this ***abussos*** is the place where the devil will be punished for 1000 years, as stated in Revelation 20:1-3. It is also the place where the demons named "legion" did not want to be cast into by Jesus, per Luke 8:30-31; thus, they were obviously familiar with it. It is also the place where the Antichrist Beast of Revelation ascends from, as recorded in Revelation 11:7 and Revelation 17:8. Therefore, we know that it is a place of punishment or torment for the devil and fallen angels or demons. It also may be the same place referred to by Peter in 2nd Peter 2:4, where angels who sinned were cast down to in "chains" of darkness. As stated previously, the word Peter used in this text, which is translated as hell, is ***tartaros***, and it is only used once in all of

Scripture. It means "deepest abyss", which would be similar to *abussos'* meaning of an abyss or pit that is bottomless. You can't get any deeper of an abyss than a bottomless one. It is also noteworthy that the angels in *tartaros* are in *chains*, and the devil will likewise be in a "great chain" in the "abussos" , per Revelation 20:1-3.

All of these things indicate that it is probably not *normal* "insect locusts" that had been locked away in this *abussos*. Furthermore, the Antichrist who also ascends from the "abussos", is certainly not a literal locust. Moreover, the king of this army of locusts is a fallen angel named Abaddon or Apollyon. Additionally, these locusts certainly do not look like normal locusts. They are shaped like horses, have faces like men, gold like crowns on their heads, hair like women's, teeth like lions', iron like breastplates and tails like scorpions. And, they sting people with their scorpion tails causing pain so intense that men desire to die. These are obviously some kind of *supernatural locusts*, and their place of origin, the *abussos*, is certainly associated with the demonic realm. Therefore, I refer to them as "demon locusts".

Revelation 9:4 stresses that these locusts of the fifth trumpet only afflict people who do not have

God's seal on their foreheads, in other words, only the wicked. This statement was not made concerning the first four trumpets, which could indicate that the first four trumpets affected everyone, including God's people. This would be similar to the plagues that God sent upon Egypt in the days of Moses, because, there also, some plagues affected both the Egyptians and the Israelites, and some only affected the Egyptians; the first three plagues affected both, but the final seven plagues affected Egyptians only. Apparently, now, from the fifth trumpet through the seventh trumpet, only the wicked are affected.

The chaos and panic caused by the first four trumpets will be multiplied greatly by the supernatural attack of these "demon locusts" with their tormenting stings. At this point, people would do anything to get relief from the calamities that have befallen them. They would gladly support any government or person who could relieve their pain and offer solutions to their problems.

The only possible remaining hindrance to Antichrist's one world government would be if America, China or Russia were able to maintain their superpower status in spite of all of the global catastrophes brought by the judgments of the first five trumpets in Revelation. However, because we know that the Bible clearly states that the Antichrist's one world government will arise; therefore, we also know that all obstacles that could stand in the way will be removed. And, accordingly, it is likely that the poisoned waters, devastating storms and catastrophic impact of the asteroid will be strategically located so as to cripple these former superpowers, reducing them to no greater status than other nations. If indeed this will be the case, that formerly mighty nations have been humbled, and all nations and peoples of earth are reeling in panic and chaos; then, the stage will have been set for the entrance of Antichrist, and for the acceptance of his one world government. The question is, "how will he enter, and why will he be viewed by all people on Earth as the one who has the solutions?"

Before I present a *possible* scenario that could cause the world to welcome Antichrist with open arms, I need to "set the stage" by reminding you that angels can impersonate human beings. The Bible states that people have unwittingly entertained angels, thinking they were strangers in need, in Hebrews 13:2. In Genesis chapter 18, the Lord and two angels appeared to Abraham as three men. And, in 1st

Samuel chapter 28, a "witch" brought up an evil spirit that appeared to be Samuel the prophet; it had to be an evil spirit, which would be one of Satan's fallen angels, because we know that witches do not have authority to make righteous dead people appear before them. Therefore, the Bible clearly reveals that angels can impersonate people.

I also need to point out the great increase in "UFO" sightings in recent decades. Informed Bible students know that civilizations from other galaxies are not visiting our wicked planet. And, although government officials try to explain all of these sightings away, to avoid mass panic and hysteria; yet, we know that there have been too many credible sightings from credible people with credible photographs in recent years for us to believe that nothing unusual or *supernatural* is happening. If it's not other civilizations visiting our planet, what is it? A previous acquaintance of mine once commented to me that people are not seeing "UFO's", but rather "UF<u>A</u>'s", unidentified "fallen angels". And, quite frankly, I think that he was correct. If this is true, why has Satan been doing this so frequently in recent decades? What is he trying to prepare us for with all of these *apparent* "UFO" visitations? Keeping this in mind, I need to share the results of recent polls done over the past 25 years regarding the subject of UFOs and aliens from other worlds visiting our planet. Polls done by, or reported by, National Geographic, the New York Post, Newsweek, 20th Century Fox, the Huffington Post, Sky News, Roper, CNN and Time Magazine, report that anywhere from 36% to 75% of American adults believe in UFOs and alien life, which is an average of 55% of adults in the United States. Television channels are filled with programs about aliens and the paranormal. It is also noteworthy that many of today's respected evolutionary scientists endorse the idea of *panspermia*; the theory that life on earth was **seeded** from "outer space" by a super intelligent race. In other words, the majority of *"everyday Americans"* and numerous scientists believe that UFOs and super intelligent **alien life forms** do exist, and that they have visited our world in the past, as well as in our present time.

Keeping all of these things in mind, I ask you to consider the following ***"possible"*** scenario. At this critical and desperate point in Earth's history, following the devastating effects of the five trumpets, which have probably already resulted in hundreds of millions of fatalities, and multitudes more beginning to die from thirst, starvation and disease; this added to the financial collapse of national economies throughout the world, and the painful torment caused by the stinging "demon locusts"; at this critical moment Earth's satellites begin receiving intelligible messages from outer space. Super intelligent beings are telling Earth's leaders and scientists that they are aware of the crisis on Earth, and that they are willing and able to help.

Because of the desperate and rapidly deteriorating conditions throughout the world, permission is given them to land on Earth and to meet with world leaders. The inhabitants of the space craft say that they will land in Rome, Italy. Media cameras from every nation are present as the spaceship lands and opens its doors. Then, the visitors appear, and everyone is in shock. Standing before them is one who appears to be the leader, and who identifies himself as Jesus Christ, but who is actually the Antichrist of Revelation chapter 13. Beside him, stands one who appears to be second in authority; he identifies himself as the prophet Mohammed, but who is really the "False Prophet" of Revelation 16:13. Other famous, religious *holy men* are also present, with one claiming to be Moses, another claiming to be the "Supreme Buddha", and also a revered and famous Hindu swami. Professed Christians, Jews, Muslims, Hindus and Buddhists, constituting nearly eighty percent of Earth's population, are filled with excitement and awe. The Antichrist explains that many roads lead to heaven, and that all are loved by God. He also states that they have landed in Rome because it is the home of the Vatican and papacy, which he states is the head of the Christian Church on Earth, thus endearing himself to the pope and to Earth's more than one billion Catholics.

The Antichrist says that he understands if some are skeptical about him. So, he offers to give proof of his power, authority and goodwill. He raises his hand and commands the tormenting *locusts* to immediately vanish throughout the world; of course, they do so because they are actually demons under his command. This instantaneous and undeniable miracle, which brings worldwide relief to every unsaved person, from the nagging persistent pain caused by these *demon locusts*; this miracle causes universal acceptance and adoration of Antichrist and his fellow demonic impersonators. However, Antichrist's "performance" has only begun. He has arranged for an assassin to be among the dignitaries welcoming his group to Earth.

And, in the midst of the festivities, he is fatally stabbed with a sword. There is pandemonium as he is pronounced dead at the scene. However, three days later his *deadly wound is healed*, as stated in Revelation 13:3, and he miraculously resurrects himself from the dead after having already been embalmed. He is able to do this because he had never truly died, for you cannot kill a demon with a sword.

Following this second incredible and undeniable miracle, the "fake" Moses instructs all Jews to worship this *false Christ*. The False Prophet, Mohammed, commands all Muslims to worship him as well. And, the "Supreme Buddha" and the *Hindu swami* follow suit, by telling all Buddhists and Hindus to also revere him. The vast majority of the world population then demands that their leaders accept and exalt Antichrist to the position of *president* or *premier* of a new worldwide government.

As I have twice stated, I present this as a *"possible"* scenario for the arrival of Antichrist. And, I think that it is not too "far-fetched", due to the extreme emphasis on UFOs, aliens and the paranormal in our contemporary culture.

Chapter Four

Armageddon and the Mark of the Beast

In Revelation 13:16-17, the Apostle John states, "(16) He causes all, both small and great, rich and poor, free and slave, to receive a *mark* on their right hand or on their foreheads, (17) and that no one may buy or sell except one who has the mark or the name of the beast, or the number of his name."

The book of Revelation clearly states that the Antichrist will force everyone throughout the world to receive a "mark" in their right hand or forehead, which they will need in order to *buy and sell*; this "mark" is commonly referred to as *the mark of the beast*. What is this *mark*? This word, "mark", is translated from the Greek word "charagma", which means *mark*, *stamp*, *etch*, *scratch*, or *engrave*. In the context of this passage in Revelation chapter 13, with this mark, etching, scratching or engraving happening to a human hand or forehead, it would seem to imply a piercing of the skin, perhaps such as would be necessary to insert a "computer microchip".

With today's technology, a computer microchip can be easily implanted in a moment's time as a nonsurgical procedure. And, in fact, thousands of people in Sweden have already had such microchips implanted in their hands. These microchips could contain all vital and legal identification, such as medical, financial, and other government required information, which would completely eliminate the need for drivers licenses, insurance cards, credit cards, checking accounts, cash, and just about all other forms of paperwork. And, according to Revelation 13:16-18, these microchips will also contain either the name of the Antichrist Beast or the number of his name, which is 666. If they contain his number, 666, it will probably be mixed in with some type of long serial number to be less conspicuous. These microchips will certainly also have satellite tracking capacity in order to effectively monitor the buying and selling of the worldwide population, as foretold in Revelation 13:16-17.

There will be numerous logical reasons given for the necessity of implanting these microchips. They will be advertised as being the means for stopping kidnapping and runaway children, because the location of all people would be known at all times. The microchips would also stop all monetary and identity theft, because they would completely eliminate the use of currency and identification documents. They would stop all illegal drug sales, because they would have created a cashless society with all transactions done via the microchips, and with all of these transactions constantly visible to government officials everywhere. Moreover, this worldwide *around the clock* monitoring of every single person would drastically reduce all other forms of crime, for it would be impossible to commit any crime without being caught immediately, because, as previously mentioned, everyone's exact location would be known at all times.

Even as I am writing this book, yet another compelling reason for microchip implantation has surfaced. As nations throughout the world are battling a worldwide pandemic, COVID-19, and hundreds of thousands of people will probably perish from this virus, many nations are discussing the need to be able to track the people who are infected with this virus. There are some nations that have already begun the tracking of these people via their cell phones. And, other countries are also considering adopting this strategy. There have even been some in America who have recommended that our nation begin such tracking. Of course, it won't be long until these countries will realize that the tracking of cell phones is not super effective, because people can avoid such tracking by simply not taking their cell phones with them when they leave their homes. It will quickly become obvious that a tracking device is needed that is **with**, **on** or **in** the people at all times. And, it will soon become apparent that the most sure way to make certain that these tracking devices have to always go with them, will be to make these devices an actual part of their bodies, by inserting them inside of each person. We will probably not see such measures adopted for this COVID-19 pandemic, at least certainly not on a worldwide basis, because nations are learning that this virus is not as deadly as it was first feared to be. However, when a future pandemic arises, which it will, that is far more contagious and much more deadly than COVID-19, and tens of millions of people are perishing throughout the world; when such a pandemic arises, nations will not just be talking about tracking cell phones. They will be insisting on a far more thorough form of tracking that cannot be escaped by those who are infected, which will require that the tracking device be placed "within" the bodies of the infected ones. This, of course, will be 100% effective for worldwide monitoring of the disease. And, the highly touted success of this "tracking" program, will then **warm people up** to the idea of microchip implantation, which will prepare the way for the ultimate worldwide tracking and monitoring plan implemented by Antichrist; the global requirement that every person in every nation on Earth must be implanted with a microchip in their right hand or forehead, as stated in Revelation chapter thirteen. As mentioned in the previous paragraph, there will be numerous *seemingly* logical, wise, compelling and necessary reasons given for this worldwide monitoring program via the insertion of these microchips into every human being on this planet. Furthermore, the convenience of not having to carry around anymore credit cards, debit cards, checks, cash, insurance cards, various licenses and other identification documents, will certainly be attractive to most people as well. It will, in fact, appear that only stubborn, unreasonable, ignorant and evil people would oppose this apparently good and necessary legal requirement of global microchip implementation.

We will now switch our attention and focus to the subject of "Armageddon". The term "Armageddon" is associated with the great final battle on earth before the return of Jesus Christ. Is it a battle between men and nations, with nations attacking each other, nations attacking Israel, and nations even attacking Antichrist, as is taught by most prophecy teachers?

From the time of mankind's original compromise with sin in the Garden of Eden, has Earth's "true" great conflict been a struggle between men, or has it been a struggle between good and evil? Has the real controversy been between nations, or has it been between God and Satan? Was it not "Lucifer", Satan's name in heaven before he sinned, who said that he wanted to exalt his own throne above the stars of God; moreover, who said that he wanted to be like the "Most High"? Note the following scripture.

In Isaiah 14:12-14, God said, "(12) How you are fallen from heaven, O Lucifer, son of the morning! How you are cut down to the ground, you who weakened the nations! (13) For you have said in your heart: "I will ascend into heaven, *I will exalt my throne above the stars of God*; I will also sit on the mount of the congregation on the farthest sides of the north; (14) I will ascend above the heights of the clouds, *I will be like the Most High*."

Lucifer (Satan) wanted to be God! In fact, the Bible records that the "first war" was fought in Heaven between God's holy angelic forces and Satan with his "fallen" angelic army. Note the following passage.

In Revelation 12:7-9, the Bible states, "(7) And *war broke out in heaven*: Michael and his angels fought with the dragon; and the dragon and his angels fought, (8) but they did not prevail, nor was a place found for them in heaven any longer. (9) So the great dragon was cast out, that serpent of old, called the Devil and Satan, who deceives the whole world; he was cast to the earth, and his angels were cast out with him."

So, according to the Bible, the "true" war started in Heaven with Lucifer's (Satan's) rebellion against God. And, after Satan's defeat in Heaven, he was cast down to Earth, which became his new battlefront against God and His Son, Jesus Christ. While on earth, Satan continued his battle against God and Jesus by causing the fall of Adam and Eve in the Garden of Eden. He then furthered his war by tempting and attacking God's Old Testament nation of Israel, and causing their apostasy. And, when Jesus came to this Earth, Satan mercilessly and brutally assaulted, harassed, tortured and crucified our Savior. After Jesus' resurrection and ascension to Heaven, Satan has continued to cruelly tempt, torment, afflict and martyr the disciples of Jesus Christ. Satan knows that Jesus said, in Matthew 25:40, that whatever is done to His "brethren", Christians, is also done to Jesus Himself. Therefore, Satan assaults Christ's followers, knowing that he is also attacking Jesus when he attacks them.

This epic conflict between God and Satan, between good and evil, has always been the "true" battle or war ever since Lucifer rebelled in Heaven. And, it will eventually culminate with one final, enormous "last stand" by Satan when Jesus returns to Earth. Note the following text.

In Revelation 16:12-16, the Apostle John said, "(12) Then the sixth angel poured out his bowl on the great river Euphrates, and its water was dried up, so that the way of the kings from the east might be prepared. (13) And I saw three unclean spirits like frogs *coming* out of the mouth of the dragon, out of the mouth of the beast, and out of the mouth of the false prophet. (14) For they are spirits of demons, performing signs, *which* go out to the kings of the earth and of the whole world, to gather them to ***the battle of "that great day of God Almighty"***. (15) "Behold, I am coming as a thief. Blessed *is* he who watches, and keeps his garments, lest he walk naked and they see his shame." (16) And they gathered them together to the place called in Hebrew, ***Armageddon***."

Per this scripture, the Antichrist Beast marshals all of the evil kingdoms and armies on earth to a place in Israel called "Armageddon". This battle or war is called the **"battle of that great day of God Almighty"**. Most prophecy teachers refer to it as the "Battle of Armageddon". This "incorrect name" and *incorrect focus* regarding this final war at Christ's return, has resulted in erroneous teachings about this "battle" by most contemporary so-called prophecy experts. They focus on the nations involved in this battle, and on the location of the battle, Armageddon, but they forget what the battle is all about. It is not about disagreements between men and nations. This battle is the culmination of the same "war" that started in Heaven, when Lucifer rebelled against God. That is why the Bible does not call it the "battle between nations" or the "battle over Israel" or the "battle of Armageddon", but rather, Scripture calls it the **"battle of that great day of God Almighty"**, in Revelation 16:14. It is the final culmination of the war between God and Satan, of the war between good and evil.

The book of Revelation clearly contradicts the teachings of today's prophecy "scholars". They teach that this so-called "Battle of Armageddon" is a great final war between nations fighting one another, nations fighting against Israel, and nations even fighting against the Antichrist. However, their teaching blatantly contradicts the book of Revelation. Note the three following verses.

In Revelation 13:3 and Revelation 13:7-8, John stated, "(3) And I saw one of his heads as if it had been mortally wounded, and his deadly wound was healed. And *"all" the world* marveled and *followed the beast*. (7) It was granted to him to make war with the saints and to overcome them. And *authority was given him over "every" tribe, tongue and nation*. (8) *"All" who dwell on the earth will worship him*, whose names have not been written in the Book of Life of the Lamb slain from the foundation of the world."

These three verses clearly state that "**all**" of the world and "**all**" who dwell on Earth will follow and worship the Antichrist Beast, and that the Antichrist will have authority over *"every" nation*. The "only ones" who will not follow him will be the ones whose names are written in the Lamb's "Book of Life", which would be Christ's disciples.

So, according to Scripture, "**all**" of the wicked will follow the Antichrist in unison, and *every nation* will be under his authority; they will **not** be fighting against him. The book of Revelation makes it clear that the Antichrist will have "total control" over, and the "full support" of, **all** of the wicked people and nations on Earth. The nations will **not** be fighting each other, they will **not** be fighting against Israel, and they will **not** be fighting against the Antichrist. What is being taught by the vast majority of today's prophecy teachers and preachers is totally, 100% unscriptural. Who will the nations be fighting? The following scriptures will prove that all of the nations on Earth will be in unison, prepared to fight against our Lord Jesus Christ when He returns. Note the two following scripture passages.

In Revelation 17:12-14, the Bible states, "(12) The ten horns which you saw are ten kings who have received no kingdom as yet, but they receive authority for one hour as kings with the beast. (13) These are of one mind, and they will give their power and authority to the beast. (14) *These will make war with the Lamb*, and the Lamb will overcome them, for He is Lord of lords and King of kings; and those *who are* with Him *are* called, chosen, and faithful."

This passage stated that the kings of the Earth and the Antichrist Beast will make war with the Lamb (Jesus). According to this text, the kings of the Earth will **not** be fighting each other, they will **not** be fighting against Israel, and they will **not** be fighting against the Antichrist; they will all be in unison with the Antichrist in his war against Jesus Christ.

In another passage in Revelation the Apostle John is given a graphic vision of this final conflict between Jesus Christ and the Antichrist, with all the armies on Earth accompanying him in his audacious plan to make war with Jesus Christ and the armies of heaven. I encourage you to read Revelation 19:11-21.

This passage depicts this final epic battle between the Antichrist Beast and Jesus Christ when He returns. Jesus is pictured as being on a white horse leading the armies of Heaven, who are clothed in white linen and who also are mounted on white horses. Revelation 19:19 unequivocally states that the Antichrist Beast along with *the kings and armies of the Earth* will be gathered together to make war "against Jesus" and His heavenly army. This text clearly portrays all of the armies on Earth being gathered in unison to fight against Jesus Christ, **not** to make war against each other, **not** to make war against Israel, and **not** to make war against Antichrist. As Revelation 16:14 stated, this is indeed the final **"battle of that great day of God Almighty"**.

How could the world's armies be so deceived and deluded to actually attack Jesus Christ when He returns? It will be because of the satanic, supernatural miracles that will be done by the Antichrist Beast and his "false prophet". Note the following scriptures.

In 2nd Thessalonians 2:9-10, the Apostle Paul declared, "(9) **The coming of the "lawless one" (Antichrist) is according to the working of Satan, with all power, "signs", and "lying wonders"**, (10) **and with all "unrighteous deception"** among those who perish, because they did not receive the love of the truth, that they might be saved."

In Revelation 13:11-14, John proclaimed, "(11) Then I saw **"another beast" (the false prophet)** coming up out of the earth, and he had two horns like a lamb and spoke like a dragon. (12) And he exercises all the authority of the first beast in his presence, and causes the earth and those who dwell in it to worship the first beast, whose deadly wound was healed. (13) **He performs "great signs", so that he even makes "fire come down from heaven" on the earth in the sight of men.** (14) **And he deceives those who dwell on the earth by those signs** which he was granted to do in the sight of the beast, telling those who dwell on the earth to make an image to the beast who was wounded by the sword and lived."

In Revelation 16:13-14, John said, "(13) And I saw three unclean spirits like frogs *coming* out of the mouth of the dragon, out of the mouth of the beast, and out of the mouth of the false prophet. (14) **For they are spirits of demons, "performing signs"**, *which* go out to the kings of the earth and of the whole world, to gather them to the battle of that great day of God Almighty."

The passage in 2nd Thessalonians mentioned the "lawless one" in verse nine, which is an obvious reference to the Antichrist, because 2nd Thessalonians 2:3-4 also calls this entity the "man of sin" and the "son of perdition". Moreover, it stated that this entity claims to be God. In 2nd Thessalonians 2:9-10, Paul stated that the Antichrist will perform *signs and wonders* with all unrighteous deception.

The Revelation 13:11-14 text said that the "being" called, "another beast", who is also called the "false prophet" in Revelation 16:13, will do *great signs*, even *making fire come down from heaven*. And, this scripture stated that those who dwell on the Earth will be deceived by those signs.

The Revelation 16:13-14 passage mentioned that "demonic spirits" will come out of the mouths of the *dragon*, the *Antichrist Beast*, and the *false prophet*, and will perform *signs* which will seduce and influence the "kings of the Earth" and the *whole world* to gather for this final battle against God, Jesus Christ, and His angelic army.

Through these miraculous signs, mentioned in these three scriptures, wicked men and nations will be deceived to believe that the Antichrist himself is indeed the true god. Thus, they will make their stand with him, and will join him in his audacious plan to fight against Jesus Christ and the armies of heaven when Jesus returns.

Scripture clearly reveals that the "Battle of Armageddon" being taught by most so-called prophecy *experts*, where the nations of Earth are fighting with each other, fighting against Israel, and even fighting against Antichrist; **the Bible reveals that this "Battle of Armageddon" doctrine clearly contradicts Scripture, and is totally, 100% unbiblical**.

If you would like to contact me regarding anything that I have discussed in this book, I would be happy to hear from you. My email address is Godormen@gmail.com. I do respond to every email that I receive. May God bless you and guide you into truth in your study of the Scriptures.

"I encourage you to place your faith in Jesus Christ as your personal Savior, if you have not already done so. Confess your sins to Him and ask Him to forgive you, and He will do so. Then surrender your entire life to Him as your Lord, and He will radically change your life for the better. You will never regret it. Everything else is empty, hollow, and meaningless, if you do not personally know Jesus as your Savior and Lord."

Other Books by Henry Bechthold

Babylon Is Fallen: "Come Out Of Her My People": The Apostasy Of The Contemporary Christian Church And Revelation 17's "Impure Woman" Revealed

Are You "All In"?: Are You Sure You Are A Follower Of Christ?

Depression in the Bible: The Biblical Strategies, Lessons and Spiritual Warfare Revealed

Anxiety, Panic Attacks, Fear and Phobias: The Biblical Solution

Antichrist, Armageddon, and the Mark of the Beast: Antichrist's Identity Revealed

Sexual Lust in the Church, Pornography, Sexual
Fantasies, Fornication and Adultery: The Biblical
Answer—You Can be Free

The Israel Deception: The Scriptures They Don't
Want You To See Revealed

The Glorious Gospel of Jesus Christ

Preterism A False Doctrine: Removing the Blessed
Hope of Christ's Return

God's Judgment On America: Abortion, Evolution,
And The Gay Agenda

ABOUT THE AUTHOR

My name is Henry Bechthold. I am a non-denominational Christian pastor. I have been preaching and teaching God's Word for the past forty years. The scriptural views and doctrines that I espouse come from my personal study of God's Word in the Bible. When it comes to biblical doctrine, the traditions and opinions of man are of no importance. I will take one plain "thus saith the Lord" over a thousand human and denominational traditions. I am of the same mindset of the disciples of Jesus, who told the unfaithful and disobedient religious leaders of their day that they "ought to obey God rather than men".

Feel free to contact me at GodorMen@gmail.com.

Printed in Great Britain
by Amazon

36049846R00057